Pastor Donald C. Carlson
Memorial Library

NORMANDALE LUTHERAN CHURCH   EDINA, MN 55436

STILL GOING BANANAS

by Charles Keller

illustrated by Hallie Coletta

Prentice-Hall, Inc.
Englewood Cliffs, New Jersey

To: Fran
Sheri
Barbara

Library of Congress Cataloging in Publication Data
Keller, Charles.
Still going bananas.
SUMMARY: A collection of jokes and riddles illustrated with line drawings.
1. American wit and humor. 2. Wit and humor, Juvenile. 3. Riddles—Juvenile literature. [1. Jokes 2. Riddles] I. Coletta, Hallie, 1951- II. Title.
PN6163.K45   817′.54′08   80-10236
ISBN 0-13-846832-X

Copyright © 1980 by Charles Keller
Illustration copyright © 1980 by Hallie Coletta

All rights reserved. No part of this book may be reproduced in any form or by any means, except for the inclusion of brief quotations in a review, without permission in writing from the publisher.
Printed in the United States of America J
Prentice-Hall International, Inc., London
Prentice-Hall of Australia, Pty. Ltd., North Sydney
Prentice-Hall of Canada, Ltd., Toronto
Prentice-Hall of India Private Ltd., New Delhi
Prentice-Hall of Japan, Inc., Tokyo
Prentice-Hall of Southeast Asia Pte. Ltd., Singapore
Whitehall Books Limited, Wellington, New Zealand
1 2 3 4 5 6 7 8 9 10

I hear you have an easy job at the watch factory. What do you do?

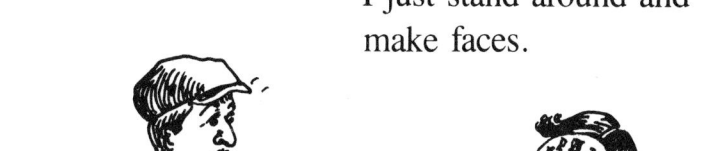

I just stand around and make faces.

- (Foreman to worker)
  How come you're only carrying two bricks, while the others are carrying four?
  I guess they're too lazy to make two trips.

- I'm homesick.
  But don't you live at home?
  Yes, and I'm sick of it.

- What's that piece of string tied around your finger for?
  My mother put it there to remind me to mail a letter.
  And did you mail it?
  No. She forgot to give it to me.

- What do they make shoes out of?
  Hide.
  What?
  Hide, hide, the cow's outside.
  Why? I'm not afraid of a cow.

- The brain is a wonderful thing.
  Why do you say that?
  It starts working the minute you
  get up in the morning and never
  stops until you're called on in class.

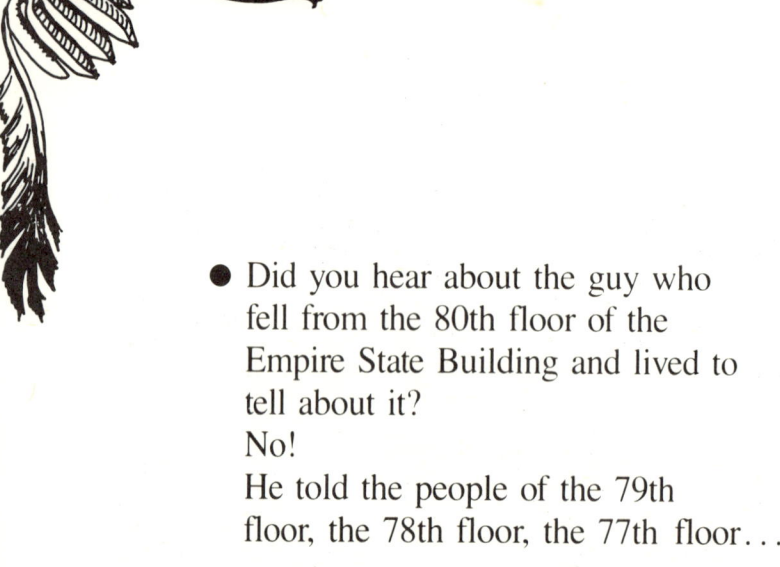

- Did you hear about the guy who fell from the 80th floor of the Empire State Building and lived to tell about it?
No!
He told the people of the 79th floor, the 78th floor, the 77th floor...

- You know the price of candy keeps going up, but the bars keep getting smaller and smaller. We should go into the candy business; we could make a mint.

Is this hair tonic any good?

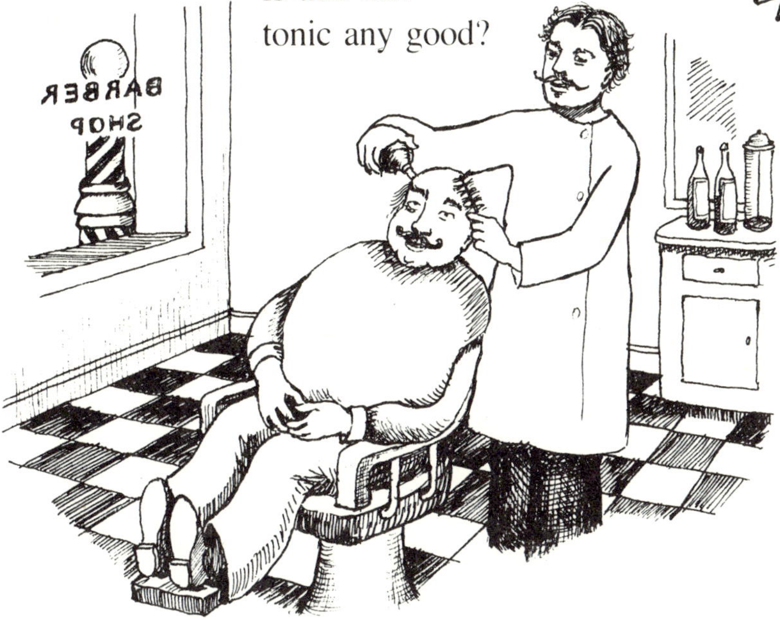

This hair tonic is so good that I spilled some on a comb and it turned into a brush.

- What kind of bird is that?
  A gulp.
  I never heard of a gulp.
  It's like a swallow, only bigger.

- (Man on telephone)
  Hello, is this the weather bureau?
  Yes, it is.
  What are the chances for a shower tonight?
  It's OK with me–take one if you need one!

Miss, I'd like to buy another ticket to the movies.

That's the third ticket you've bought. Why are you buying so many?

Because some man inside keeps ripping them up.

- (Man at dentist's office)
  Good heavens! You've got the
  biggest cavity I've ever seen!
  Ever seen! Ever seen!
  You don't have to repeat yourself!
  I didn't. That was an echo!

- Are you sure this dog you're
  selling me is loyal?
  I'll say he is. I've sold him five
  times and every time he came back.

Why are you eating
bananas with the skin on?

It's all right.
I know what's inside.

3) When I want to find out what time it is in the middle of the night I sit down and start playing my piano. The neighbors then shout, "It's four o'clock in the morning. Stop playing that stupid piano."

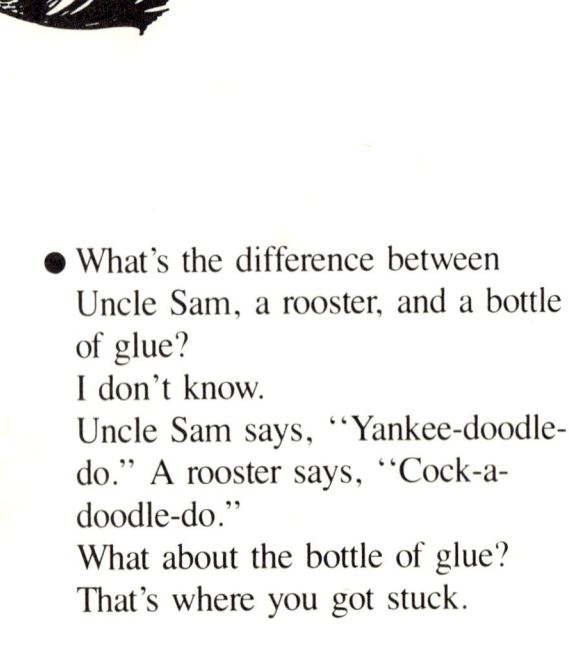

- What's the difference between Uncle Sam, a rooster, and a bottle of glue?
  I don't know.
  Uncle Sam says, "Yankee-doodle-do." A rooster says, "Cock-a-doodle-do."
  What about the bottle of glue?
  That's where you got stuck.

- What are you looking for in that mud?
  I heard it rained an inch and three quarters last night, and I'm looking for the quarters.

I once grew a beard like yours but when I saw how terrible it made me look I shaved it off.

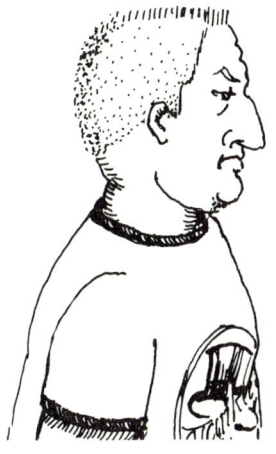

I used to have a face like yours, too, but when I saw how terrible it made me look I grew a beard.

- My sister is so smart she is only
  in the first grade and can spell her
  name backwards.
  Really! What's her name?
  Anna.

- Doctor, I can't sleep.
  Did you try counting sheep?
  Yes, I counted up to 125,000.
  Then you fell asleep?
  No, then it was time to get up.

My electric toaster broke
so I repaired it with parts
from an old airplane.

How does it work?

Not badly; except that when the toast pops up it
circles the table twice before coming in for a landing.

- Where are you going with that watering can?
  Out to water the plants.
  But it's raining out.
  So I'll wear my raincoat.

- (Tourist to man on country road)
  This is a steep drop-off. Why don't you put up a fence and a danger sign?
  We did have a sign up once, but nobody fell off so we took it down.

- Could you lend me $2 so I can see my family?
  Certainly, where is your family?
  At the movies.

- Do you know what happens on a clear day in southern California?
  No, what?
  U.C.L.A.

1) Johnny, what was that crash?

2) Mom, you know that antique glass bowl that you were always worried about me breaking?

3) Yes.

Well, your worries are over.

- (Customer to paperboy)
  Do you mind if I pay you in pennies?
  Of course not! Do you mind if I deliver your newspaper one page at a time?

- What does it mean when the barometer starts falling?
  I guess it means that whoever nailed it up didn't do a good job.

Do you have any experience in acting?

Sure—my leg was in a cast once!

- (Delivering groceries)
  What's your name?
  Frank Sinatra.
  My, that's a well-known name!
  It should be, I've been delivering groceries in this neighborhood for two years.

- When I was a little boy I always ate my spinach.
  Did you like it?
  Of course, I did.
  Good, then you can have mine.

- What are the people in New York noted for?
  Their stupidity.
  Where did you get that idea?
  It says in the book that the population of New York is very dense.

- When is your birthday?
  March 15.
  What year?
  Every year.

Doctor, I get a sharp pain in my eye every time I drink coffee. What should I do?

Try taking the spoon out of the cup.

- Animals are definitely smarter than people.
  Why do you say that?
  Well, if you put 10 horses in a race, thousands of people would go to see it, but if you put 10 people in a race, not one horse would go to see it.

It will be twenty dollars
for two questions.

Isn't twenty dollars a lot of money
for only two questions?

Yes, it is. Now, what was
your second question?

1) How was your horseback riding yesterday?

2) Not so good. My horse was too polite.

3) Too polite?

4) Yes, when we came to a fence he let me go first.

- I was seeing funny spots before my eyes so I got a pair of eyeglasses.
Did they help?
Sure. I can see the spots much clearer now.

How many feet are there in a yard?

It depends on how many people are standing in it.

- (Lady to butcher)
  Those sausages you sold me were meat at one end and corn meal at the other.
  Lady, in hard times like these it's hard to make both ends meat!

- My father wants me to have everything he didn't have when he was a boy.
  What didn't he have?
  All A's on his report card.

Waiter, this lobster has only one claw.
Yes sir, that proves how fresh our lobsters are. They fight with each other in the kitchen.
Well, go back in the kitchen and bring me a winner.

- (Man to bank employee)
  I'd like to borrow some money.
  I'm sorry, sir, but the loan
  arranger isn't in today.
  That's OK, I'll talk to Tonto.

I heard you played hookey from school today and played baseball.

No, mom, and I have the fish to prove it.

- I'm going to watch "The Green Monster from the Red Swamp" on television tonight.
Don't you mean "The Red Monster from the Green Swamp?"
It doesn't matter. I have a black-and-white set.

Do ships this size sink very often?

No, only once.

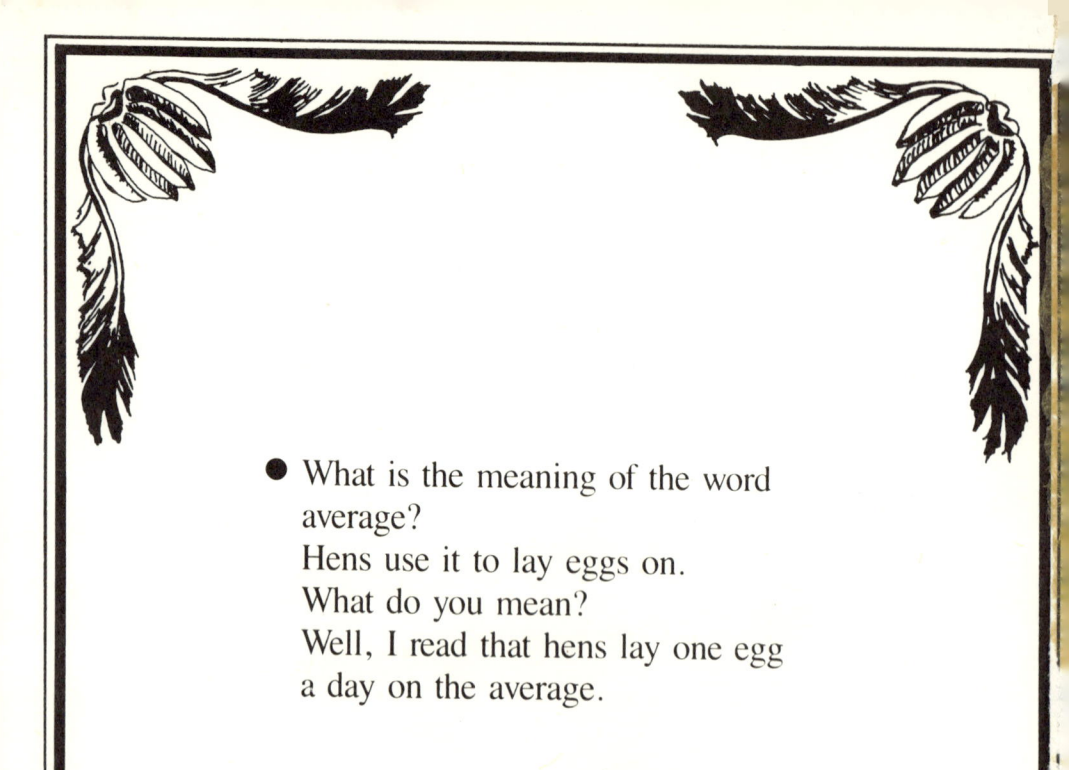

- What is the meaning of the word average?
  Hens use it to lay eggs on.
  What do you mean?
  Well, I read that hens lay one egg a day on the average.

- Last night I put a tooth under my pillow and this morning I found a dime in its place.
  I put mine under a pillow and got a dollar.
  Wow–you must have had a buck tooth.

B 5126
Keller, Charles
STILL GOING BANANAS
AUTHOR
TITLE

B 5126
Keller, Charles
STILL GOING BANANAS

NO

CARLSON MEMORIAL LIBRARY
NORMANDALE LUTHERAN CHURCH
6100 NORMANDALE ROAD
EDINA, MN 55436